A Thousand Goodbyes

A Thousand Goodbyes

Taye Carrol

A Thousand Goodbyes

Copyright © 2024 Taye Carrol

All rights reserved.

ISBN: 9798883598240

In memory of my mother
Doris Lillian Horowitz Frank
The strongest woman I've ever known

A Thousand Goodbyes

CONTENTS

Introduction	Pg 9
A Daughter's Poem	Pg 10
In These Moments	Pg 11
Echoes of Absence	Pg 12
After Image	Pgs. 13 - 14
Broken Bonds	Pgs 15 - 16
A Distant Song	Pg 17
Adrift	Pg 18
Between Breaths	Pg 19
Perpetuity	Pgs 20 - 21
January 6, 2024	Pg 22
Bird on a Ledge	Pg 23
Longed For	Pg 24
Shared Sunsets	Pgs 25 - 26
Melancholy	Pg 27
Rainbows On a Rain-Free Day	Pgs 28 - 29
To Go Unanswered	Pg 30
The Ring	Pg 31
Guardians of Memory	Pg 32
A Love Filled Elegy	Pgs 33 - 34
About the Author	Pg 36

INTRODUCTION

The poems in this book reflect a very raw and personal account of my last days with my mother. I am sharing this in the hopes it touches familiar cords in others who have or are going through something similar. But it is a book meant for everyone, even those who haven't lost a loved one. At some point in time, the unfortunate reality is that we all will lose someone we care very deeply about. It is how the world works. For those who haven't lost someone yet, let the words inspire you to draw those you love close. Take the time now to appreciate all they contribute to your life and share that with them. You never want to look back and wish you had.

A Daughter's Poem

In the quiet cradle of my heart
A dance unfolds, tender and unseen
Where thoughts twirl like dandelion seeds
Each one a fleeting fragment of you

Like the gentle flutter of butterfly kisses
Your essence flits across the stage
A momentary ballet in the theater of memory
Where the heart is both spectator and dancer

In this choreography of the soul
Where each thought is a graceful movement
The music of unspoken tenderness
Resonates in the corridors of shared silence

In These Moments

In the fading glow of twilight
Mother and daughter linger
As memory's canvas stirs
Gentle strokes of a daughter's love
Unspoken words dance
Forever in their steps

Gestures become verses
Unlimited by syntax
Eyes become poets
Stanzas etched in glances
A silent language growing
Profound, eternal, nuanced

We stroll hand in hand
Through gardens of shared yesterdays
Each step resonates
With yet unborn refrains
A pebble rippling outward
The silence sings its own song

In the realm where language falters
The heart's whisper reigns supreme
A masterpiece created
In the quiet midnights
Of shared togetherness
An eternal universe born

Echoes of Absence

In the solitude of distance, a child engages in a tacit conversation with an ailing parent, transcending the miles that stretch like an infinite expanse. The profound dialogue unfolds, not in spoken words, but in the quiet spaces outside of time where emotions echo.

Across the vastness, a spectral conversation ensues, traversing the realm of sentiments unspoken. The weight of impending loss hovers, a silent symphony of unexpressed thoughts weaving through the corridors of absence.

Time becomes an elusive companion, slipping through the fingers like sand, as the child explores the intangible threads connecting hearts across the spatial void. In the silence, a poignant narrative emerges, tracing the contours of an inevitable farewell.

The language of the soul, intricate and nuanced, manifests in the unspoken gestures of love that bridge the physical gap. A canvas of emotions unfurls, painted with hues of longing, acceptance, and the quiet resilience born from the impending departure.

Each moment becomes a microcosm of shared existence, a delicate dance between presence and impending absence. The child navigates this enigmatic landscape of emotions, seeking solace in the echoes that reverberate across the vast emptiness, creating a living mosaic of sentiments too profound for language.

In the space of gathering silence, the child and parent embark on a journey of connection that transcends the limitations of physical separation. The dance of unspoken emotions, the eloquence of shared glances, and the resonance of unsaid words become the lyrical notes in the symphony of farewell.

Afterimage

In the quiet expanse of bygone moments,
a distant silhouette, the form of a mother,
fades into the dwindling light of days past.
A delicate dance, an unraveling
of sepia threads, a creation spun
by the persistent flow of temporal currents.

Her presence, a play of touch,
fingers brushing against the substance of ages,
the tactile melody of shared existence
imbued in the core of maternal atmosphere.
Yet, like the elusive strains of a night song,
she withdraws, a figure in the throat
of the hourglass's relentless rhythm,
the rhythmic pulse of ceaseless seconds.

Silhouette outlined against the sheer veil
of days painted in subdued hues, where shadows
become familiar with the outlines of memories.
The senses, once bound to her embrace,
now tethered to the echo of her vacancy,
a lingering scent, a hushed melody
hummed by the breeze of fleeting years.

In the vestibule of retrospection,
her voice echoes, a melodic murmur
whispering through the passages of remembrance.
A symphony of laughter, the rhythm
of admonishments, a gaze's affirmation,
A moment's approval
a composition written in the heart's ink.

(Afterimage cont.)

And yet, the daughter, a traveler through eras,
watches as the illusion of maternal presence
fades, as the prism of the essence
into glimpses of what was,
a montage etched with the threads
of joy and sorrow, marked in the chamber
of filial consciousness.

The space between now and then,
a void that swallows the tangible,
leaving only the intangible residue
of a presence unfurling into absence.
A silhouette against the radiant canvas
of what is, what was, what endures
in the shifting chamber of memory's keep

Broken Bonds

In the quiet of familial shadows, where unspoken secrets stretch like echoes, a daughter stands sentinel to the profound ache of vigil-keeping. No melodic orchestration of comfort graces this space; instead, the air is heavy with the stifled breath of unuttered grief. The daughter, a solitary wanderer, crosses the dusk of despair, footsteps muffled by the weight of struggles that cling to the walls.

The sounds of her solitude become a solemn presence, a muted rhythm of sorrow. The daughter's heart beats in a timorous cadence, the only audible pulse in this realm of familial indifference. The vigil keeper assumes a role akin to a lone lifeline, etching her silhouette against the backdrop of night.

In the design of grief's intricate pattern, the daughter grapples with ashen echoes — supposed allies offering no true solace, mere specters haunting the edges of empathy. Like fleeting dreams, harmony eludes this quietude, drowned in the dirge that reverberates through the emptiness.

Alone, beneath the moon's stoic gaze, the vigil becomes a personal narrative etched against the stark truth painted in tones of deepest black.

The daughter's world is colored with threads of desolation, a story of pain emerging in the dim corners of her heart. Empathy remains unvoiced, and the vigil becomes a journey with shadows, an experience of one, an elegy echoing in the emptiness.

(Broken Bonds cont.)

In the frigid stillness, where the heart contends with the weight of grief, a requiem unfolds — not in harmonic convergence but in the disarray of emotions left unattended. The daughter, a phantom etched in the absence of familial warmth, carries the burden of vigil-keeping, a choice made in the quiet spaces where tears are the only witnesses.

Yet, within the quiet, a revelation emerges — solitude's grip, though firm, yields to the shared salvation found in the compassionate embrace of kindred souls. The daughter's solitary vigil, a transient experience in the familial realm of grief, finds its denouement in the company of those who share in the tender understanding of her story even in the absence of those who should care.

A Distant Song

In the hush between heartbeats
A sanctuary unfurls, unnamed
Where solitude becomes a sacred canvas
Upon which memories paint in whispers

No orchestration of words
No narratives woven in spoken tones
But tales remembered clothed in silent resonance
That reaches through the corridors of absence

In stillness an invisible presence aligns
A daughter's breath, a far-off sigh
Tracing the silence's gentle curves
Rich with shared outlines, one atop one

Within the hush, a daughter searches for solace,
Seeking a haven untouched by tumult,
A sanctum serene where memories aren't tarnished
But arrayed in soft hues, genuine and honest

Not a cosmic dance of sun, stars and moon
But a subtle choreography of constant emotion
Each quiet reflection a celestial movement
A constellation mapped in the daughter's quiet gaze

In the silence the daughter finds not emptiness,
but depth, a presence cloaked in the unassuming
A testament to the enduring beauty
That resides in the spaces beyond spoken words

Adrift

A stillness settles around me
An empty echo resounding in these final languid days
I grasp at motes floating through fading light
Futile fists full of dust
Memories sway like willows in this barren mind
Their once-green branches now skeletal, trembling
I dare not dwell beneath their cold shadows
pace fast-beating heart rates around this small room
Seeking, turning, stopping short at each forced admiration
"How bright gleams that glinting picture frame"
"A most lovely pattern on this porcelain bowl"
"The red of the glass such a nice shade against the cherry wood"
But wander too near shattered shards of a former life
Glittering knife-edges threatening to slice open
Half-healed wounds of a heart turned ashen about to be orphaned.
I stand solitary, staring out darkened windows
At faint stars pricked through the gloom.
No candles here
To light a passage forward
After the last flicker fades

Between Breaths

In the dim-lit room where time hangs heavy,
Mother and daughter share a silent instant
Their breaths syncopated, a delicate rhythm
Each inhale a whisper of existence
Each exhale a release of the past

Between the pauses, introspection blooms
A garden of memories, tangled and wild
The daughter's hand reaches out
Grasping at fragments of a fading reality
While the mother drifts, untethered

Words become obsolete in this sacred space
Where the quiet speaks volumes
Echoing the unsaid, the unfinished
The daughter's heart aches with the weight of unspoken truths
And the mother, she listens with eyes closed

In the stillness, time loses its grip
And they exist in the eternity of the moment
Wrapped in a cocoon of shared breaths
Where love transcends the boundaries of the physical
And the hush between breaths becomes their language

Perpetuity

In the quiet expanse where the physical begins to unravel, the daughter discerns the subtle melody of whispers. She stands at the meeting point of the seen and unseen, where the wind plays orator, articulating secrets carried from distant spheres.

The tender breeze, messenger of a cosmic lexicon, unfurls narratives with careful fingers, a spectral dance, decipherable only by the heart attuned to the frequencies of the intangible. The daughter, ever the celestial alchemist, distills the breeze into momentary verses, transmuting air into the ink of connection.

Each murmur bears the imprints of the mother's presence, clandestine conversations etched upon the invisible manuscript of the surrounding space. The daughter, with senses honed to the harmonies of the unseen, absorbs these poetic exhales, words formed not by vocal cords but by the resonance of ephemeral strings.

In the rustle of leaves, the daughter perceives stanzas of counsel, the evanescent choir imparting the wisdom of a lifetime of seasons. The breeze, a master calligrapher, sketches impermanent runes, leaving traces of love and guidance upon the daughter's contemplative brow.

With eyes closed, the daughter discerns the song of rustling grasses, an intimate ballad sung by the sagacious choir. The wind, the unseen minstrel, plays upon her face, a sonorous caress orchestrating a concerto of tender reminiscence.

The daughter, at the threshold of conjoined realms, translates these whispers into the cadence of her own existence. The air, now adorned with the ambrosial scent of recognition, binds them in an intangible embrace, a dance of interconnected breaths.

(Perpetuity cont.)

As the daughter listens to the soft hymn of the breeze, she uncovers a universe of untold tales, where love metamorphoses into the dialect of the unseen, where each murmur is a testament to an unbroken bond. Through this metaphysical parlance, the daughter discovers the ineffable truth that love, woven into the very fabric of the unseen, becomes a perennial murmur—subtle, perpetual, and eternally beautiful. She internalizes the gift, aged and ageless, and it is hers and hers alone.

January 6, 2024

In the quiet folds of sorrow's rent garment
Tears cascade, gentle as lingering embraces
Each drop a testament to the ache within
A language spoken in the silent eloquence of grief

Embraces that linger, like dew on morning petals
A soft touch of remembered warmth
Tracing the contours of a love once tangible
Now etched in the dampened trails of sorrow

They fall, not in defeat, but as warriors weeping
Warriors of the heart, clad in vulnerability
Each tear a residue of an embrace unforgotten
A whisper of love lingering on the skin of despair

And in those tear-stained moments
The heart cradles the weight of memories
As if embracing the shadows of what was
Ad what now exists in the sacred realm of absence

Tears, the artistry of the soul
Painting portraits of joy and loss
Mingling with the echoes of laughter
In the sacred dance of emotions untamed

Bird on a Ledge

In the stillness before dawn's tender breath, where sorrow's veil hangs heavy and profound, I stand as a sentinel of grief by the windowpane. Lost amidst the vast expanse of a world without her, my spirit echoes with the hollow resonance of loss, a tempest of fractured memories swirling within and all around me.

Amid the shadows of desolation, a solitary figure emerges from the mist. A bird, draped in the silken shroud of twilight's embrace, alights upon the ledge, a steadfast witness to my mourning. Its song, a fragile melody of solace, pierces through the breathless silence, offering a flicker of hope amidst the darkness.

With each new morning, it returns before the light, constant and unwavering, a silent guardian in the kingdom of sorrow. Its wings, a symphony of grace and resilience, beat against the weight of the darkness, a beacon of light in the depths of my despair. Day after day, it dances upon the threshold, a testament to the endurance of the human spirit, a reminder of life's eternal flame.

And as I stand, bathed in the soft glow of morning's light, I feel the weight of her absence heavy upon my soul. Yet in the gentle cooing of the winged messenger, I find a glimmer of solace, a fleeting moment of peace within the storm. For in the ebb and flow of grief's relentless tide, there lies a promise of renewal, a reminder that love endures, eternal and unyielding, even in the darkest of hours.

Longed For

In the sacred grove of memory, an ancient oak, weathered and wise, cradles whispers of a love that defies words. Its branches, like a mother's arms, reach out to the heart that aches with longing. Shadows, like delicate dancers in the fading twilight, twirl in a dance that mirrors the once-vibrant spirit, painting the world in hues of life.

The phoenix's journey, a mystical tale, tells of a flight through challenges, rebirth through fire and obstacles witnessed by tearful stars weeping at what seemed inevitable, yet never before was. A harvest of golden memories, gathered from fields where laughter once ripened, now stands as a tribute to a life well lived – a bounty the grieving child holds close, though for now it remains just out of reach.

In the unsolvable labyrinth of absence, the steadfast oak murmurs stories of endurance, yet the child, a melancholic wanderer in this hallowed space, craves the tangible warmth of a vanished touch. Shadows dance not in high spirits but in a tender elegy for an unfinished melody. The phoenix's song, once triumphant, now lingers in the heart's soft chambers, a haunting melody woven into the fabric of departure.

The endless warmth of deep southern days, once a crown of plenty, seems distant to the bereaved, an abundance of memory too heavy to bear alone. In the moonlit legacy, the child seeks solace, yearning for the intangible embrace of a lost part of herself. Longing becomes a gentle breeze, rustling through the leaves of the steadfast oak, whispering a poignant ode to the fleeting nature of love, and the infinite nature of love eternal.

Shared Sunsets

Within twilight's gentle arms, we gather
A family etched in the delicate filigree
Of sunsets, moments unbridled, a collective of shared breaths

No crafted patterns against the lyrical flow of seconds
Each heartbeat mingling in the essence of existence
Anchored by the radiant pulse of family

The sun, an alchemist's gold sinking beneath the edge
Painting the firmament in hues of saffron and rose
In this quiet theater, we seek refuge

Discourses unfold like petals of a summer rose (gardenia)
The silhouettes of laughter etched against the waning light
The sun's descent, a parable for life's transient course

Warmth lingers, not just in the evening's parting goodbye
But in the nuanced lexicon of shared words, unspoken bonds
Shared sorrows touched with the brushstrokes of understanding

As the sun gives way to night's insistence
We stand, silhouetted against the canvas of dimming light,
An homage to the enduring impression left by our departed matriarch

Gratitude, a silent companion amidst the shadows,
A profound acknowledgment of life's poignant choreography.
In absence, sunsets emerge as testimonials to love's enduring eloquence

(Shared Sunsets cont.)

Her dream exists, is here
The comfort, the strength, the resilience
The ability to tolerate what we never thought we could
Seeing that one alone is powerless but all together
There is nothing that can't be done

Everything is family

Melancholy

In burnt sunsets' embrace,
Echoes of longing linger,
Lost in hues of sorrow,
Fading into oblivion's sigh.

Rainbows On a Rain-Free Day

In the vast expanse of flawless sky
Where forecasts falter and rain sleeps silent
Moments of radiant intricacies emerge
Eclipses of colored light
Against whisps of pure white clouds

Not the usual archetypal spectrum,
But a freestyle formation manifest
Colors intermingling in defiance of tradition
A testament, perhaps, to the reimagining of perspective
For even rainbows, unconfined, find form in the unexpected

Against the perfect white the colors materialize
As if a message for us alone
Not bound by arcs but expressions undefined
Free yet bound halfway between
A permanent connection beneath their transient facade

They hover, not in solitude, but in collaboration,
Each hue against the backdrop of unblemished clouds
Which permits perception, pulls the eye above the trees
And the clouds against a backdrop of cerulean sky
Without which the prism might fail to catch the eye

The radiant intricacies softened tell a story
Of hopes unanticipated, reshaped yet still fulfilled
A reminder for us perhaps
That all dreams are possible
Though not always exactly as predicted

(Rainbows On a Rain-Free Day cont.)

In the dance of colors against the canvas of clouds
Emotions take form, and values find expression
As the blue sky supports the clouds
and the clouds the rainbows
so do the ones who love us see the truth that lies within

To Go Unanswered

In the quiet hollow of night, she reaches out, but solitude beckons.
Fingers linger over buttons
A portal to vanished cadence, a void of echoes
Words unsaid dissolve into shadows
Drifting like smoke through the void of absence
Silent confessions writhe on the gnarled bark of longing
Unspoken requiems lost in time
Grief, a cosmic sorrow, etched in stardust
A lullaby of tears sung to uncharted constellations

The Ring

In the stillness of her days, she holds a memory
Twisted in silver, a spiral of heartbeats whispered
Facets of light, each diamond a story told
In the hush of her mother's last breaths

The large stone, a beacon of presence
Reflects the time shared in shadows and light
In the quiet spaces where grief and joy entwine
She's comforted by the familiar sight that now rests on her hand

She watches the dance of rainbows thrown wide, finding solace
In the ever-turning spiral of remembering
A daughter's heart, heavy with the weight of loss
Lifted by the radiance of a mother's love, enduring

Guardians of Memory

In the realm of the Guardians of Memory,
Where ancient giants roam with regal grace,
There lies a lesson whispered by the wind,
A parable of honor in the whispers of loss.

Within the shadows of the somber trees,
The elephants gather in a solemn dance,
Their steps a testament to enduring love,
Their very presence a lesson in lament.

In each footfall, a tale of time's passage,
Echoes of bygone days imprint the earth,
Their tusks, like monuments to yesterday,
A reminder of the unraveling of days.

Their vigil kept with stoic devotion,
A reverie of remembrance amidst the dusk,
Each heartbeat a rhythm of resilience,
A symphony of solace in the guise of grief.

Mourning silhouettes against the fading light,
They paint a portrait of beauty from bereavement,
A tapestry woven with threads of sorrow,
A poignant reminder of life's fragile dance.

In the realm of the Guardians of Memory,
Where sorrow sings with the wind's gentle sigh,
The elephants stand as stoic teachers,
Their wisdom woven in whispers of goodbye.

A Love Filled Elegy

In dawn's rosy fingers, I feel your caress
An infinite tenderness that transcends the waking sky
Not in the tangible touch of finite hands
But in the hue of endless beginnings

On the palette of memory, you paint
With the brushstrokes of whispered echoes
Across the canvas of fleeting moments
Where time bends to cradle our shared history

In the sun's gilded grasp, a radiant mirror
A perpetual glow unscathed by the cool breath
Of temporal parting, where love outshines the passing days

In the embrace of gentle winds, a hint of fragrance
Not of petals or perfume, but nostalgia's ambered notes
The sensory poetry of life-filled recollection
Unfurling like petals in the quiet meadows of remembrance

Though you reside elsewhere now
I still hear your voice whispering in the wind's breath
A dulcet refrain that entwines with the threads
Of a symphony, unheard but felt, conducted by an ageless maestro

And that which is felt but unseen, the tactile
Traces chills, warmth filled, across my skin
As I taste the bittersweet pain of longing
A flavor that lingers just beyond the tip of perception

(A Love Filled Elegy cont.)

You gave me the horizon, an infinite arc of possibility
Bearing witness to the expansiveness of love within hardship
Stretching across the ley lines of existence
A boundless expanse where boundaries dissolve

In the crystalline gaze of stars, your watchfulness
A cosmic sentry overlooking the eternity of night
A silent guardian of our shared moments
As constellations etch our story in star-studded calligraphy

All together they form a sonnet
Composed in the language of absence
Here but not here
Gone but not gone
And so across the arc of time, you will remain
My beginning, my ending, my always

I love you, Mom.

A Thousand Goodbyes

ABOUT THE AUTHOR

Taye Carrol is a psychologist by training, and a fiction and poetry writer by choice. Her short stories and poetry have been featured in Siren's Call, Haunted Waters Press, Weirdbook Magazine, Zero Fiction, Haiku Hub and Dead Poets Live among others. She serves as Managing Editor (Serials, Novellas) for LVP Press and is Editor in Chief for Mental Gecko and Promposity, both of which she founded. She is about to release her new poetry collection, "A Thousand Goodbyes", which traces the journey between mother and daughter over the course of her mother's final weeks.

Made in the USA
Columbia, SC
27 July 2024